The Gettysburg Address: The History and Legacy of President Abraham Lincoln's Greatest Speech

By Charles River Editors

A picture of Lincoln (being pointed at by the red arrow) and the crowd for the dedication

About Charles River Editors

Charles River Editors provides superior editing and original writing services across the digital publishing industry, with the expertise to create digital content for publishers across a vast range of subject matter. In addition to providing original digital content for third party publishers, we also republish civilization's greatest literary works, bringing them to new generations of readers via ebooks.

Sign up here to receive updates about free books as we publish them, and visit Our Kindle Author Page to browse today's free promotions and our most recently published Kindle titles.

Introduction

The Gettysburg Address

"Four score and seven years ago our fathers brought forth on this continent a new nation, conceived in liberty, and dedicated to the proposition that all men are created equal. Now we are engaged in a great civil war, testing whether that nation, or any nation so conceived and so dedicated, can long endure. We are met on a great battlefield of that war. We have come to dedicate a portion of that field, as a final resting place for those who here gave their lives that that nation might live." – Abraham Lincoln

Without question, the most famous battle of the American Civil War took place outside of the small town of Gettysburg, Pennsylvania, which happened to be a transportation hub, serving as the center of a wheel with several roads leading out to other Pennsylvanian towns. From July 1-3, Robert E. Lee's Confederate Army of Northern Virginia tried everything in its power to decisively defeat George Meade's Union Army of the Potomac, unleashing ferocious assaults that inflicted nearly 50,000 casualties in all.

After the South had lost the war, the importance of Gettysburg as one of the "high tide" marks of the Confederacy became apparent to everyone, making the battle all the more important in the years after it had been fought. While former Confederate generals cast about for scapegoats, with various officers pointing fingers at Robert E. Lee, James Longstreet, and James Stuart, historians and avid Civil War fans became obsessed with studying and analyzing all the command decisions and army movements during the entire campaign. Despite the saturation of coverage, Americans refuse to grow tired of visiting the battlefield and reliving the biggest battle fought in North America.

When a crowd came to Gettysburg in November 1863 to commemorate the battle fought there 4 months earlier and dedicate a new national cemetery, they came to hear a series of speeches about the Civil War and the events of that battle. Today it may seem obvious to invite the president to such an occasion, but Lincoln was initially an afterthought, and though he did come to deliver remarks, he was not in fact the keynote speaker. Instead, the man chosen to give the keynote speech was Edward Everett, a politician and educator from Massachusetts. Everett had already been a Congressman, the 15th Governor of Massachusetts, Minister to Great Britain, and Secretary of State, and by the Civil War, he was considered perhaps the greatest orator in the nation, making him a natural choice to be the featured speaker at the dedication ceremony.

Everett is still known today for his oratory, but more for the fact that he spoke for over two hours at Gettysburg immediately before President Lincoln delivered his immortal two-minute Gettysburg Address. Everett would later say, "I should be glad if I could flatter myself that I came as near to the central idea of the occasion, in two hours, as you did in two minutes." At the time, however, Lincoln and many others present at the event thought his speech fell flat and was ultimately a failure that would be consigned to the dustbin of history.

Perhaps Lincoln's most impressive feat is that he was able to convey so much with so few words; after Everett spoke for hours at Gettysburg, Lincoln's Gettysburg Address only took a few minutes, but in those few minutes, Lincoln invoked the principles of human equality espoused by the Declaration of Independence. In the process, he redefined the Civil War as a struggle not merely for the Union but as "a new birth of freedom" that would bring true equality to all of its citizens, ensure that democracy would remain a viable form of government, and would also create a unified nation in which states' rights were no longer dominant.

150 years later, Lincoln's speech is still considered arguably the greatest in American history, yet the exact wording of the speech is disputed. The five known manuscripts of the Gettysburg Address differ in a number of details and also differ from contemporary newspaper reprints of the speech. In fact, at the time, few Americans knew the president had even given a speech at Gettysburg, and the Gettysburg Address was not widely covered in newspapers. The irony is lost on few, given that the Gettysburg Address continues to represent a concise and eloquent

statement on the very purpose of the United States.

The Gettysburg Address: The History and Legacy of President Abraham Lincoln's Greatest Speech chronicles the history of the speech from its origins to its legacy. Along with pictures of important people, places, and events, you will learn about the Gettysburg Address like never before, in no time at all.

The Gettysburg Address: The History and Legacy of President Abraham Lincoln's Greatest Speech

About Charles River Editors

Introduction

    Chapter 1: The Battle of Gettysburg

    Chapter 2: Planning a Dedication

    Chapter 3: Writing the Speech

    Chapter 4: Lincoln in Gettysburg

    Chapter 5: Delivering the Speech

    Chapter 6: Reactions to the Speech

    Chapter 7: The Real Climax of All American Eloquence

    Chapter 8: Different Versions

Online Resources

Bibliography

Chapter 1: The Battle of Gettysburg

The Battle of Gettysburg is rightly remembered as being one of the Civil War's pivotal events, but it has taken on such a reputation as the war's biggest battle and crucial turning point that it is often viewed out of the context of the rest of the war. Regardless of whether some historians and others interested in the Civil War attach too much significance to it, Gettysburg was not fought in a vacuum, and the major battle that immediately preceded it had a great effect on some of the leading generals' decisions in Pennsylvania.

At the start of 1863, Confederate general Robert E. Lee had concluded an incredibly successful year for the Confederates in the East. Having taken command in June 1862, Lee led the Army of Northern Virginia to victory over George McClellan's Army of the Potomac in front of Richmond in the Peninsula Campaign, decisively defeated John Pope's Army of Virginia at the Second Battle of Bull Run, fought McClellan's Army of the Potomac to a tactical draw (but strategic defeat) in Maryland at Antietam, and inflicted a decisive defeat on Burnside's Army of the Potomac at Fredericksburg.

Lee

However, entering 1863 the Confederacy was still struggling. The Confederate forces in the West had failed to win a major battle, suffering defeat at places like Shiloh in Tennessee and across the Mississippi River. As the war continued into 1863, the southern economy continued to deteriorate. Southern armies were suffering serious deficiencies of nearly all supplies as the Union blockade continued to be effective as stopping most international commerce with the

Confederacy. Moreover, the prospect of Great Britain or France recognizing the Confederacy had been all but eliminated by Lincoln issuing the Emancipation Proclamation in the wake of Antietam.

Given the unlikelihood of forcing the North's capitulation, the Confederacy's main hope for victory was to win some decisive victory or hope that Abraham Lincoln would lose his reelection bid in 1864, and that the new president would want to negotiate peace with the Confederacy. Understandably, this colored Confederate war strategy, and unquestionably Lee's.

In the spring of 1863, General Lee discovered that General George McClellan had known of his plans and was able to force a battle at Antietam in 1862 before all of General Lee's forces had arrived. General Lee now believed that he could successfully invade the North again, and that his defeat before was due in great measure to a stroke of bad luck. In addition, General Lee hoped to supply his army on the unscathed fields and towns of the North, while giving war ravaged northern Virginia a rest. After Chancellorsville, Corps commander James Longstreet and Lee met to discuss options for the Confederate Army's summer campaign. Longstreet advocated detachment of all or part of his corps to be sent to Tennessee, citing Union Maj. General Ulysses S. Grant's advance on Vicksburg, the critical Confederate stronghold on the Mississippi River. Longstreet argued that a reinforced army under Bragg could defeat Rosecrans and drive toward the Ohio River, compelling Grant to release his hold on Vicksburg. Lee, however, was opposed to a division of his army and instead advocated a large-scale offensive (and raid) into Pennsylvania. In addition, General Lee hoped to supply his army on the unscathed fields and towns of the North, while giving war ravaged northern Virginia a rest.

Knowing that victories on Virginia soil meant little to an enemy that could simply retreat, regroup, and then return with more men and more advanced equipment, Lee set his sights on a Northern invasion, aiming to turn Northern opinion against the war and against President Lincoln. With his men already half-starved from dwindling provisions, Lee intended to confiscate food, horses, and equipment as they pushed north--and hopefully influence Northern politicians into giving up their support of the war by penetrating into Harrisburg or even Philadelphia. Given the right circumstances, Lee's army might even be able to capture either Baltimore or Philadelphia and use the city as leverage in peace negotiations.

After their victories at Fredericksburg and Chancellorsville against armies twice their size, Confederate troops felt invincible and anxious to carry the war north into Pennsylvania. As it turned out, the Confederates would blindly stumble into the Union Army of the Potomac outside of Gettysburg on July 1, 1863, and the first day of the battle by itself would have been one of the 25 biggest battles of the Civil War. The first day ended with a tactical Confederate victory, and Union casualties were almost 9,000, while the Confederates suffered slightly more than 6,000. But the battle had just started, and thanks to the actions of commander George Meade and one of his corps commanders, Winfield Scott Hancock, the largest battle on the North American continent would take place on the ground of their choosing.

On the morning of July 2, Meade was determined to make a stand at Gettysburg, and Lee was determined to strike at him. That morning, Lee decided to make strong attacks on both Union flanks while feinting in the middle, ordering Ewell's corps to attack Culp's Hill on the Union right while Longstreet's corps would attack on the Union left. Lee hoped to seize Cemetery Hill, which would give the Confederates the high ground to harass the Union supply lines and command the road to Washington, D.C. Lee also believed that the best way to do so would be to use Longstreet's corps to launch an attack up the Emmitsburg Road, which he figured would roll up the Union's left flank, presumed to be on Cemetery Hill. Lee was mistaken, due in part to the fact Jeb Stuart and his cavalry couldn't perform reconnaissance.

As it turned out, both attacks ordered by Lee would come too late. Though there was a controversy over when Lee ordered Longstreet's attack, Longstreet's march got tangled up and caused several hours of delay. Lost Cause advocates attacking Longstreet would later claim his attack was supposed to take place as early as possible, although no official Confederate orders gave a time for the attack. Lee gave the order for the attack around 11:00 a.m., and it is known that Longstreet was reluctant about making it; he still wanted to slide around the Union flank, interpose the Confederate army between Washington D.C. and the Army of the Potomac, and force Meade to attack them. Between Longstreet's delays and the mixup in the march that forced parts of his corps to double back and make a winding march, Longstreet's men weren't ready to attack until about 4:00 p.m.

Ultimately, it was the occupation and defense of Little Round Top that saved the rest of the Union line at Gettysburg. Had the Confederates commanded that high ground on the Union left, it would have been able to position artillery that could have swept the Union lines along Cemetery Ridge and Cemetery Hill, which would have certainly forced the Army of the Potomac to withdraw from their lines. The 20th Maine's Joshua L. Chamberlain would be awarded the coveted Congressional Medal of Honor for "daring heroism and great tenacity in holding his position on the Little Round Top against repeated assaults, and carrying the advance position on the Great Round Top", and the 20th Maine's actions that day became one of the most famous attacks of the Battle of Gettysburg and the Civil War as a whole.

Ewell's orders from Lee had been to launch a demonstration on the Union right flank during Longstreet's attack, which started at about 4:00 p.m. as well, and in support of the demonstration by Hill's corps in the center. For that reason, Ewell would not launch his general assault on Culp's Hill and Cemetery Hill until 7:00 p.m.

While the Army of the Potomac managed to desperately hold on the left, Ewell's attack against Culp's Hill on the other end of the field met with some success in pushing the Army of the Potomac back. However, the attack started so late in the day that nightfall made it impossible for the Confederates to capitalize on their success. Due to darkness, a Confederate brigade led by

George H. Steuart was unaware that they were firmly beside the Army of the Potomac's right flank, which would have given them almost unlimited access to the Union army's rear and its supply lines and line of communication, just 600 yards away.

That night, Meade held another council of war. Having been attacked on both flanks, Meade and his top officers correctly surmised that Lee would attempt an attack on the center of the line the next day. Moreover, captured Confederates and the fighting and intelligence of Day 2 let it be known that the only Confederate unit that had not yet seen action during the fighting was George Pickett's division of Longstreet's corps.

Longstreet did not meet with Lee on the night of July 2, so when Lee met with him the following morning he found Longstreet's men were not ready to conduct an early morning attack, which Lee had wanted to attempt just as he was on the other side of the lines against Culp's Hill. With Pickett's men not up, however, Longstreet's corps couldn't make such an attack. Lee later wrote that Longstreet's "dispositions were not completed as early as was expected."

On the morning of July 3, the Confederate attack against Culp's Hill fizzled out, but by then Lee had already planned a massive attack on the Union center, combined with having Stuart's cavalry attack the Union army's lines in the rear. A successful attack would split the Army of the Potomac at the same time its communication and supply lines were severed by Stuart, which would make it possible to capture the entire army in detail.

There was just one problem with the plan, as Longstreet told Lee that morning: no 15,000 men who ever existed could successfully execute the attack. The charge required marching across an open field for about a mile, with the Union artillery holding high ground on all sides of the incoming Confederates. Longstreet ardently opposed the attack, but, already two days into the battle, Lee explained that because the Army of the Potomac was here on the field, he must strike at it. Longstreet later wrote that he said, "General Lee, I have been a soldier all my life. It is my opinion that no fifteen thousand men ever arrayed for battle can take that position." Longstreet proposed instead that their men should slip around the Union forces and occupy the high ground, forcing Northern commanders to attack them, rather than vice versa.

A picture of the field of Pickett's Charge taken from the Union Line near the High Water Mark. The ridge of trees is where the Confederate Line was positioned.

Realizing the insanity of sending 15,000 men hurtling into all the Union artillery, Lee planned to use the Confederate artillery to try to knock out the Union artillery ahead of time. Although old friend William Pendleton was the artillery chief, the artillery cannonade would be supervised by Porter Alexander, Longstreet's chief artillerist, who would have to give the go-ahead to the charging infantry because they were falling under Longstreet's command. Longstreet was certain of failure, but Pickett and the men preparing to make the charge were confident in their commanders and themselves.

Eventually, Union artillery chief Henry Hunt cleverly figured that if the Union cannons stopped firing back, the Confederates might think they successfully knocked out the Union batteries. On top of that, the Union would be preserving its ammunition for the impending charge that everyone now knew was coming. When they stopped, Lee, Alexander, and others mistakenly concluded that they'd knocked out the Union artillery.

A short time later, the Confederates were prepared to step out for the charge that bears

Pickett's name, even though he commanded only about a third of the force and was officially under Longstreet's direction. Today historians typically refer to the charge as the Pickett-Pettigrew-Trimble Assault or Longstreet's Assault to be more technically correct. Since A.P. Hill was sidelined with illness, Pettigrew's and Trimble's divisions were delegated to Longstreet's authority as well. To make matters worse, Hill's sickness resulted in organizational snafus. Without Hill to assign or lead troops, some of his battle-weary soldiers of the previous two days were tapped to make the charge while fresh soldiers in his corps stayed behind.

Thus, about 15,000 Confederates stepped out in sight and began their charge with an orderly march starting about a mile away, no doubt an inspiring sight to Hancock and the Union men directly across from the oncoming assault. Pickett launched his attack as ordered, but within five minutes the men came to the top of a low rise where his line came into full view of Union defenses.

As the Confederate line advanced, Union cannon on Cemetery Ridge and Little Round Top began blasting away, with Confederate soldiers continuing to march forward. One Union soldier later wrote, "We could not help hitting them with every shot . . . a dozen men might be felled by one single bursting shell." By the time Longstreet's men reached Emmitsburg Road, Union artillery switched to firing grapeshot (tin cans filled with iron and lead balls), and as the Confederate troops continued to approach the Union center, Union troops positioned behind the wall cut down the oncoming Confederates, easily decimating both flanks. And while some of the men did manage to advance to the Union line and engage in hand-to-hand combat, it was of little consequence.

Today Pickett's Charge is remembered as the American version of the Charge of the Light Brigade, a heroic but completely futile march that had no chance of success. In fact, it's remembered as Pickett's Charge because Pickett's Virginians wanted to claim the glory of getting the furthest during the attack in the years after the war. The charge suffered about a 50% casualty rate while barely making a dent in the Union line before retreating in disorder back across the field. Pickett's post-battle report was apparently so bitter that Lee ordered it destroyed.

While nobody questions that Meade's strategy at Gettysburg was strong, he was heavily criticized by contemporaries for not pursuing Lee's army more aggressively as it retreated. Chief-of-staff Daniel Butterfield, who would call into question Meade's command decisions and courage at Gettysburg, accused Meade of not finishing off the weakened Lee. Meade would later state that as his army's new commander, he was uncertain of his troops' capabilities and strength, especially after a battle that had just resulted in over 20,000 Union casualties. Moreover, heavy rains made pursuit almost impossible on July 4, and Lee actually invited an attack during the retreat, hoping Meade would haphazardly attack strongly fortified positions.

Though historians now mostly credit Meade with making proper decisions in the wake of the battle, Lincoln was incredibly frustrated when Lee successfully retreated south. On July 14,

Lincoln drafted a letter that he ultimately put away and decided not to send to Meade, who never read it during his lifetime:

"I have just seen your despatch to Gen. Halleck, asking to be relieved of your command, because of a supposed censure of mine. I am very--very--grateful to you for the magnificent success you gave the cause of the country at Gettysburg; and I am sorry now to be the author of the slightest pain to you. But I was in such deep distress myself that I could not restrain some expression of it. I had been oppressed nearly ever since the battles at Gettysburg, by what appeared to be evidences that yourself, and Gen. Couch, and Gen. Smith, were not seeking a collision with the enemy, but were trying to get him across the river without another battle. What these evidences were, if you please, I hope to tell you at some time, when we shall both feel better. The case, summarily stated is this. You fought and beat the enemy at Gettysburg; and, of course, to say the least, his loss was as great as yours. He retreated; and you did not, as it seemed to me, pressingly pursue him; but a flood in the river detained him, till, by slow degrees, you were again upon him. You had at least twenty thousand veteran troops directly with you, and as many more raw ones within supporting distance, all in addition to those who fought with you at Gettysburg; while it was not possible that he had received a single recruit; and yet you stood and let the flood run down, bridges be built, and the enemy move away at his leisure, without attacking him. And Couch and Smith! The latter left Carlisle in time, upon all ordinary calculation, to have aided you in the last battle at Gettysburg; but he did not arrive. At the end of more than ten days, I believe twelve, under constant urging, he reached Hagerstown from Carlisle, which is not an inch over fifty-five miles, if so much. And Couch's movement was very little different.

Again, my dear general, I do not believe you appreciate the magnitude of the misfortune involved in Lee's escape. He was within your easy grasp, and to have closed upon him would, in connection with our other late successes, have ended the war. As it is, the war will be prolonged indefinitely. If you could not safely attack Lee last Monday, how can you possibly do so South of the river, when you can take with you very few more than two thirds of the force you then had in hand? It would be unreasonable to expect, and I do not expect you can now effect much. Your golden opportunity is gone, and I am distressed immeasurably because of it.

I beg you will not consider this a prosecution, or persecution of yourself As you had learned that I was dissatisfied, I have thought it best to kindly tell you why."

Still, Meade was promoted to brigadier general in the regular army and was officially awarded the Thanks of Congress, which commended Meade "... and the officers and soldiers of [the Army of the Potomac], for the skill and heroic valor which at Gettysburg repulsed, defeated, and drove back, broken and dispirited, beyond the Rappahannock, the veteran army of the rebellion."

From almost the moment the Civil War ended, Gettysburg has been widely viewed as one of the decisive turning points of the Civil War. As renowned Civil War historian described Gettysburg, "It might be less of a victory than Mr. Lincoln had hoped for, but it was nevertheless a victory—and, because of that, it was no longer possible for the Confederacy to win the war. The North might still lose it, to be sure, if the soldiers or the people should lose heart, but outright defeat was no longer in the cards." While some still dispute that labeling, Lee's Army of Northern Virginia was never truly able to take the strategic offensive again for the duration of the war.

Naturally, if Gettysburg marked an important turning point in the Civil War, then to the defeated South it represented one of the last true opportunities the South had to win the war. After the South had lost the war, the importance of Gettysburg as one of the "high tide" marks of the Confederacy became apparent to everyone, making the battle all the more important in the years after it had been fought. Former Confederate comrades like Longstreet and Jubal Early would go on to argue who was responsible for the loss at Gettysburg (and thus the war) in the following decades. Much of the debate was fueled by those who wanted to protect Lee's legacy, especially because Lee was dead and could not defend himself in writing anymore. However, on July 3, Lee insisted on taking full blame for what occurred at Gettysburg, telling his retreating men, "It's all my fault." Historians have mostly agreed, placing the blame for the disastrous Day 3 on Lee's shoulders, and Porter Alexander would later call it Lee's "worst day" of the war.

However, after the war, former Confederates would not accept criticism of Lee, and blame for the loss at Gettysburg was thus placed upon other scapegoats. Although it was not immediately apparent where the blame rested for such a devastating loss, not long after the Battle of Gettysburg two names kept surfacing: cavalry leader General "Jeb" Stuart and General James Longstreet; Stuart blamed for robbing Lee of the "eyes" he needed to know of Union movement, and Longstreet for delaying his attack on Round Top Hills the second day and acting too slowly in executing the assault on the Union left flank.

To a great extent, the Confederates' search for scapegoats is a product of the fact that they were so used to being successful that a defeat had to be explained by a Southern failure, not a Northern success. In casting about for Southern deficiencies, it is often overlooked that Meade and his top subordinates fought a remarkably efficient battle. Meade created an extremely sturdy defensive line anchored on high ground, he held the interior lines by having his army spread out over a smaller area, and he used that ability to shuffle troops from the right to the left on July 2. Moreover, Meade was able to rely on his corps commanders, especially Hancock, to properly use their discretion. Before the battle, Lee reportedly said that Meade "would commit no blunders on my front and if I make one ... will make haste to take advantage of it." If he said it, he was definitely right.

Perhaps none other than George Pickett himself put it best. When asked (certainly ad nauseam) why Pickett's Charge had failed, Pickett is said to have tersely replied, "I've always thought the Yankees had something to do with it."

Chapter 2: Planning a Dedication

"THE Battle of Gettysburg came to a close on the eve of Independence Day, 1863. The famous Gettysburg Address of Abraham Lincoln, however, was not made at the time of this important contest, and the remarks were not inspired by the militia in action. It was those brave men who had given 'the last full measure of devotion,' which drew from Lincoln the memorable words spoken on November 19, 1863, at the consecration of the Gettysburg National Cemetery. It was more than four months after the actual conflict that a part of the very field where men had fought was consecrated as a place where men were buried. The din and clamor of battle had given place to calm and quiet, and in an atmosphere charged with reverence and thoughts of the dead, the requiem pronounced by Abraham Lincoln was heard." - Louis A. Warren, *Little Known Facts About the Gettysburg Address*

In early November 1863, Abraham Lincoln received a letter that set in motion one of the defining moments of his presidency and American history as a whole. It had been written on November 2 by David Wills, who described himself as an "Agent for A.G. Curtin, Gov. of Penna. and acting for all the States." He wrote, "Sir, The Several States having Soldiers In the Army of the Potomac, who were killed at the battle of Gettysburg, or have since died at the various hospitals which were established in the vicinity, have procured grounds on a prominent part of the Battle Field for a Cemetery, and are having the dead removed to there and properly buried. These Grounds will be Consecrated and set apart to this sacred purpose, by appropriate Ceremonies on Thursday the 19th instant, - Hon Edward Everett will deliver the Oration. I am authorized by the Governors of the different States to invite you to be present, and participate in these ceremonies, which will doubtless be very imposing and solemnly impressive. It is the desire that, after the Oration, You, as Chief Executive of the Nation, formally set apart these grounds to their Sacred use by a few appropriate remarks. It will be a source of great gratification to the many widows and orphans that have been made almost friendless by the Great Battle here, to have you personally! and it will kindle anew in the breast of the comrades of these brave dead, who are now in the tented field or nobly meeting the foe in the front, a confidence that they who sleep in death on the Battle Field are not forgotten by those highest in authority; and they will feel that, should their fate be the same, their remains will not be uncared for. We hope you will be able to be present to perform this last solemn act to the Soldiers dead on the Battle Field."

Photograph of David Wills ca. 1856.

Wills

Governor Curtin

Edward Everett

It is difficult to guess what Lincoln must have felt when he received this letter. The Battle of Gettysburg, which had turned the tide of the Civil War in the Union's favor, had been a bloodbath, and while the casualty numbers are well-known, the cleanup of the area and the burial of soldiers over the coming weeks is often overlooked. The soldiers killed had been hastily buried immediately after the battle, often in unmarked mass graves, but not long after the battle ended, plans had been initiated to create a proper military cemetery on the site. According to an article carried in the *New York Tribune* in November 1863, "Soon after the memorable battle of Gettysburg, it occurred to the mind of David Wills, Esq., of this place, that if arrangements could be made for the purchase of a portion of the battle-field of Gettysburg for the purposes of a

'National Cemetery,' wherein should be placed the bodies of those of our men who fell in that battle, it would not only save a large expense in the removing of the bodies by the friends of the fallen brave, but would be something which, if rightly managed and carried out, we should all, as a nation, feel a just pride in. The idea was a good one ; for in what more appropriate place could those who so nobly fought and died for the institutions of their country and their perpetuation have than the spot where, struggling manfully and heartily, they chanced to fall? Mr. Wills, after much deliberation upon the matter, and after finding that his plan was at least feasible, had an interview with Gov. Curtin upon the subject. The Governor, who, throughout the State, is called the 'Soldier's Friend,' at once seized upon the idea, and after consultation with the Governors of the different States, ordered Mr. Wills to purchase, for the State of Pennsylvania, such ground as he might deem most suitable for the purpose. This was at once done, and some seventeen acres of land were purchased for the sum of $3,150; and arrangements were immediately made for the removing from the places where were so hastily buried after the battle, our brave Union defenders, and placing, within the grounds of the 'National Cemetery,' their hallowed remains."

By November, the stage was set to dedicate the new cemetery. The *Tribune* article continued, "From that time to the present this good work has been going on; and some six weeks since it had so far progressed as to fully prove its perfect success. It was then deemed advisable to appoint a day when the grounds so sacredly set apart should be formally consecrated with appropriate exercises. It should be mentioned here that each of the eighteen States represented at the battle, purchased portions of the grounds, and agreed with the Commonwealth of Pennsylvania that the future expense should be borne by each."

To commemorate this reburial, a special event to celebrate the Consecration of the National Cemetery at Gettysburg was planned for November 19, 1863, and Lincoln was asked to speak at it. Of course, he was not the only one, as the *Tribune* explained, "All things having thus been most satisfactorily arranged, Thursday, the 19th of this month, was fixed upon as the day of consecration; and Mr. Wills, whom Governor Curtin had previously appointed his agent, and who had also been specially selected by the other States to act for them all, through the newspapers of the land, invited all who so felt inclined, to lend their presence upon the occasion. It being considered a national undertaking, invitations were specially addressed to the Governors of all the loyal States, and various public men and notabilities."

John Nicolay, one of Lincoln's secretaries during the war, later noted, "Mr. Lincoln had a little more than two weeks in which to prepare the remarks he might intend to make. It was a time when he was extremely busy, not alone with the important and complicated military affairs in the various armies, but also with the consideration of his annual message to Congress, which was to meet early in December. There was even great uncertainty whether he could take enough time from his pressing official duties to go to Gettysburg at all. Up to the 17th of November, only two days before the ceremonies, no definite arrangements for the journey had been made."

Nicolay

Still, it seems that Lincoln was determined to go, writing to his Secretary of Treasury, Salmon P. Chase, on November 17: "I expected to see you here at cabinet meeting, and to say something about going to Gettysburg. There will be a train to take and return us. The time for starting is not yet fixed; but when it shall be I will notify you." By this time, Chase had already written to Wills declining to attend the ceremony, but in the meanwhile, the Secretary of War, Edwin Stanton, had written to Lincoln, "It is proposed by the Baltimore and Ohio road: First, to leave Washington Thursday morning at 6 A. M. Second, to leave Baltimore at 8 A. M., arriving at Gettysburg at twelve, noon, thus giving two hours to view the ground before the dedication ceremonies commence. Third, to leave Gettysburg at 6 P. M., and arrive at Washington at midnight, thus doing all in one day." Lincoln responded, "I do not like this arrangement. I do not wish to so go that by the slightest accident we fail entirely; and, at the best, the whole to be a mere breathless running of the gantlet. But any way."

Chapter 3: Writing the Speech

"IT WAS on November 2, seventeen days before the address, that the invitation to participate in the Gettysburg program reached Lincoln, and knowing his deep interest in the project, one would suggest that he immediately gave some thought to what he might say at the dedication. John Nicolay, one of his secretaries, observes that Lincoln 'probably followed his usual habit in such matters, using great deliberation in arranging his thoughts, and molding his phrases mentally, waiting to reduce them to writing until they had taken satisfactory form.' There is much difference of opinion as to when he found it convenient to write out his address, but all authorities in a position to know his movements in Washington are agreed that the first draft was written before he left the Capitol for Gettysburg. There is no dependable evidence, whatsoever, that indicates he wrote any part of the address on the way to Gettysburg. That some corrections in his manuscript were made after arriving at Gettysburg, and that the last part of it especially, was rewritten is an assured fact. The writing was done in the home of Mr. Wills where Lincoln was a guest. What is known as the battlefield revision copy is transcribed on two pieces of paper, the first part written in ink and the concluding part written in pencil." - Louis A. Warren, *Little Known Facts About the Gettysburg Address*

Since the speech itself is legendary, there are inevitably a bunch of legends concerning its composition, but at least some of the facts behind the speech's origins are understood. William H. Lambert, a well-known orator in his own right, wrote in 1909, "President Lincoln left Washington for Gettysburg at noon on Wednesday, November 18, 1863, in a special train consisting of four passenger coaches; he was accompanied by a large party that included members of his Cabinet, several foreign ministers, his private secretaries, officers of the Army and Navy, a military guard, and newspaper correspondents; the train arrived at Gettysburg about dark. Mr. Lincoln spent the night at the house of David Wills, Governor Curtin's representative and the active agent in the establishment of the Soldiers' Cemetery."

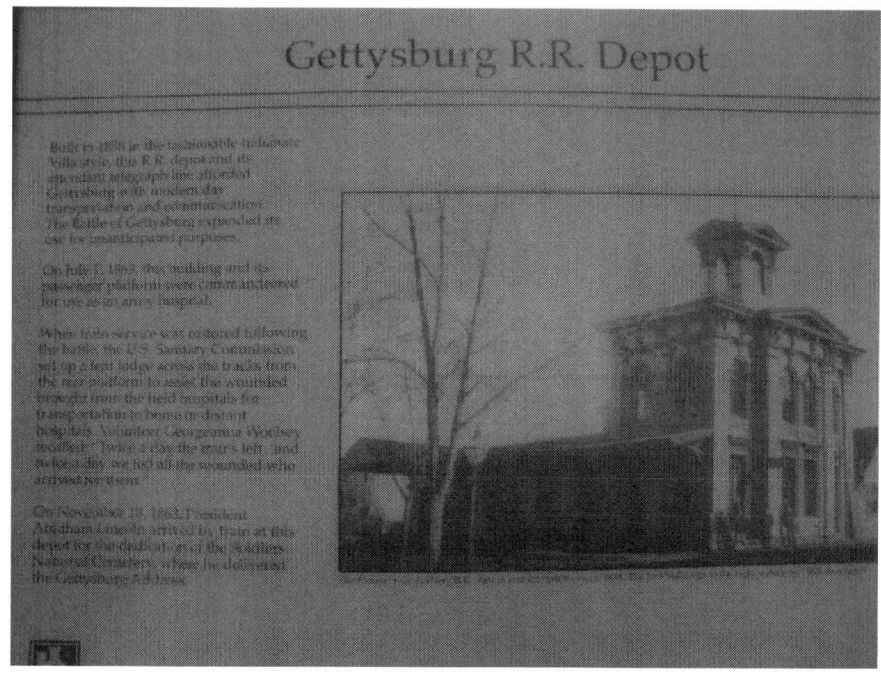

A picture of the railroad depot Lincoln used at Gettysburg

Aside from those facts, there is still an unsettled debate over some of the particulars. According to Isaac Arnold, who wrote, *History of Lincoln and the Overthrow of Slavery* in 1866, Lincoln "while on his way from the White House to the battlefield was notified that he would be expected to make some remarks," and "retiring to a seat by himself, with a pencil he wrote the address." 19th Century author Ben Perley Poore agreed, writing that "his remarks at Gettysburg…were written in the car on his way from Washington to the battlefield, upon a piece of pasteboard held on his knee."

While both these stories are charming, they are likely inaccurate; General James Fry, who was with Lincoln on the trip as an official escort, later wrote, "I have no recollection of seeing him writing or even reading his speech during the journey, in fact there was hardly any opportunity for him to read or write."

Years after the Civil War, Nicolay observed, "There is no decisive record of when Mr. Lincoln wrote the first sentences of his proposed address. He probably followed his usual habit in such matters, using great deliberation in arranging his thoughts, and molding his phrases mentally, waiting to reduce them to writing until they had taken satisfactory form. There was much greater necessity for such precaution in this case, because the invitation specified that the address of dedication should only be "a few appropriate remarks." Brevity in speech and writing was one of Lincoln's marked characteristics; but in this instance there existed two other motives calculated to strongly support his natural inclination. One was that Mr. Everett would be quite certain to make a long address; the other, the want of opportunity even to think leisurely about what he might desire to say. All this strongly confirms the correctness of the statement made by the Hon. James Speed, in an interview printed in the 'Louisville Commercial' in November, 1879, that the President told him that 'the day before he left Washington he found time to write about half of his speech.'"

William Mowry, author of *History of the United States for Schools* (1896), offered up Governor Curtin's description of events: "Governor Curtin said that after the arrival of the party from Washington, while the President and his Cabinet, Edward Everett, the orator of the day, Governor Curtin, and others were sitting in the parlor of the hotel, the President remarked that he understood that the committee expected him to say something. He would, therefore, if they would excuse him, retire to the next room and see if he could write out something. He was absent some time, and upon returning to the company had in his hand a large-sized, yellow government envelope. The President sat down, and remarked that he had written something, and with their permission he would like to read it to them, and invited them to criticize it. After reading what he had written upon the envelope, he asked for any suggestions they might make; Secretary Seward volunteered one or two comments, which Mr. Lincoln accepted and incorporated. Then he said, 'Now, gentlemen, if you will excuse me again, I will copy this off,' and returning again made a fresh copy to read from."

Seward

Judge Horatio King, who was also there that evening, told a slightly different story, claiming, "I saw Mr. Lincoln writing this address in Mr. Wills' house on a long yellow envelope. He may have written some of it before. He said 'I will go and show it to Seward,' who stopped at another house, which he did and then returned and copied his speech on a foolscap sheet."

On the other hand, Ward Lamon, a personal friend of Lincoln's, unequivocally insisted, "A day or two before the dedication of the National Cemetery at Gettysburg, Mr. Lincoln told me that he would be expected to make a speech on the occasion; that he was extremely busy, and had no time for preparation; and that he greatly feared he would not be able to acquit himself with credit, much less to fill the measure of public expectation. From his hat (the usual receptacle for his private notes and memoranda) he drew a sheet of foolscap, one side of which was closely written with what he informed me was a memorandum of his intended address. This he read to me, first remarking that it was not at all satisfactory to him. It proved to be in substance, if not in exact words, what was afterwards printed as his famous Gettysburg speech. … There is neither record, evidence, nor well-founded tradition that Mr. Lincoln did any writing, or made any notes, on the journey between Washington and Gettysburg. The train consisted of four passenger-coaches, and either composition or writing would have been extremely troublesome amid all the movement, the noise, the conversation, the greetings, and the questionings which ordinary courtesy required him to undergo in these surroundings ; but still worse would have been the rockings and joltings of the train, rendering writing virtually impossible. Mr. Lincoln carried in his pocket the autograph manuscript of so much of his address as he had written at Washington the day before. ... The whole of this first page — nineteen lines — is written in ink in the President's strong clear hand, without blot or erasure.... But when, at Gettysburg on the morning of the ceremonies, Mr. Lincoln finished his manuscript, he used a lead pencil, with which he crossed out the last three words of the first page, and wrote above them in pencil 'we here be dedica,' at which point he took up a new half sheet of paper — not white letter-paper as before, but a bluish- gray foolscap of large size with wide lines, habitually used by him for long or formal documents, and on this he wrote, all in pencil, the remainder of the word, and of the first draft."

There is another problem in trying to determine when exactly Lincoln wrote his famous speech. When he left Washington on the morning of November 18, he was coming down with what ended up being a case of smallpox. He began to notice that he wasn't feeling well that morning and mentioned an overall feeling of malaise to John Hay, one of his personal secretaries. The next morning, he confided in Nicolay that he was feeling unwell and a bit lightheaded. By the time the ceremony was over and he was back on the train, he was running a fever and complaining of a migraine headache. A few days later, he was diagnosed with smallpox, though fortunately only a mild case. Given how he was feeling, it would be all the more remarkable if Lincoln managed to craft a substantial portion of the speech despite feeling that poorly.

For his part, Lambert concluded, "Whatever revision may have been given to the Address en route to or at Gettysburg, whatever changes or additions may have been made in its delivery, the Address existed in substantially completed form before the President left Washington. There can be no doubt that he had given prolonged and earnest thought to the preparation of this Address; he had had more than two weeks' notice that he was desired to speak ; and although the demands upon his time and attention were such as to allow him little opportunity for uninterrupted thought, he appreciated the momentousness of the occasion, he knew how much was expected of him, and what was due to the honored dead, and he did not trust to the inspiration of the moment or rely upon his readiness as an impromptu speaker when he dedicated the Soldiers' Cemetery at Gettysburg, for he had wrought and re-wrought until there came into perfect form the noblest tribute to a cause and its heroes ever rendered by human lips."

Chapter 4: Lincoln in Gettysburg

"The Gettysburg program was arranged by the National Soldiers Cemetery Committee, and they selected Edward Everett as the orator for the occasion. The first date set for the exercises as Thursday, October 13, 1863, but Mr. Everett felt he could not be ready to speak so soon as that and then suggested that November 19 would be the earliest possible date on which he could appear. This date was approved. Officially, Lincoln had no voice in the plans for the celebration as it was not under the jurisdiction of the United States Government. Out of courtesy to him, however, in ample time to prepare the few remarks he was expected to make, he was invited by the committee in charge to participate in the ceremonies. This request he graciously accepted, apparently without any feeling that his invitation to be present was unduly belated, as is often alleged." - Louis A. Warren, *Little Known Facts About the Gettysburg Address*

Lincoln had only been informed of the proposed dedication ceremony 17 days before it actually took place, but he still had some influence over scheduling. According to Nicolay, "The President's criticism of the time-table first suggested must have struck Secretary Stanton as having force, for the arrangement was changed, so that instead of starting on Thursday morning, the day of the ceremonies, the President's special train left Washington at noon of Wednesday the 18th. Three members of the cabinet — Mr. Seward, Secretary of State, Mr. Usher, Secretary of the Interior, and Mr. Blair, Postmaster- General — accompanied the President, as did the French minister M. Mercier, the Italian minister M. Bertinatti, and several legation secretaries and attaches. Mr. Lincoln also had with him his private secretary Mr. Nicolay, and his assistant private secretary Colonel John Hay. Captain H. A. Wise of the navy and Mrs. Wise (daughter of Edward Everett) were also of the party; likewise a number of newspaper correspondents from Washington, and a military guard of honor to take part in the Gettysburg procession. Other parties of military officers joined the train on the way. No accident or delay occurred, and the party arrived in Gettysburg about nightfall."

When David Wills wrote to Lincoln that November, he enclosed a personal note that might seem amazing to modern readers in an era of heavy Secret Service details: "As the hotels in our town will be crowded and in confusion at the time referred to in the enclosed invitation, I write to invite you to stop with me. I hope you will feel it your duty to lay aside pressing business for a day to come on here to perform this last sad rite to our brave soldier dead, on the 19th inst. Governor Curtin and Hon. Edward Everett will be my guests at that time, and if you come you will please join them at my house."

A picture of the Wills letter to Lincoln

Lincoln took Wills up on his offer. As Nicolay later put it, "According to invitation Mr. Lincoln went to the house of Mr. Wills, while the members of the cabinet, and other distinguished persons of his party, were entertained elsewhere. Except during its days of battle the little town of Gettysburg had never been so full of people. After the usual supper hour the streets literally swarmed with visitors, and the stirring music of regimental bands and patriotic glee clubs sounded in many directions. With material so abundant, and enthusiasm so plentiful, a serenading party soon organized itself to call on prominent personages for impromptu speeches, and of course the President could not escape. The crowd persisted in calling him out, but Mr. Lincoln showed himself only long enough to utter the few commonplace excuses which politeness required."

Nicolay took it upon himself to record the president's words that day and later published them as having been the following: "I appear before you, fellow-citizens, merely to thank you for this compliment. The inference is a very fair one that you would hear me for a little while at least, were I to commence to make a speech. I do not appear before you for the purpose of doing so, and for several substantial reasons. The most substantial of these is that I have no speech to make. In my position it is somewhat important that I should not say any foolish things. [A voice: 'If you can help it.'] It very often happens that the only way to help it is to say nothing at all. Believing that is my present condition this evening, I must beg of you to excuse me from addressing you further."

The festivities continued into the evening and evolved into something of a political meeting. Nicolay reported, "The crowd followed the music to seek other notabilities, and had the satisfaction of hearing short speeches from Secretary Seward, Representatives McPherson and McKnight, Judge Shannon, Colonel John W. Forney, Wayne MacVeagh, and perhaps others. These addresses were not altogether perfunctory. A certain political tension existed throughout the entire war period, which rarely failed to color every word of a public speaker, and attune the ear of every public listener to subtle and oracular meanings. Even in this ceremonial gathering there was a keen watchfulness for any sign or omen which might disclose a drift in popular feeling, either on the local Pennsylvania quarrel between Cameron and Curtin, or the final success or failure of the Emancipation Proclamation; or whether the President would or would not succeed himself by a re-nomination and reelection in the coming campaign of 1864. There were still here and there ultra-radical newspapers that suspected and questioned Seward's hearty support of the emancipation policy. These made favorable note of his little address in which he predicted that the war would end in the removal of slavery, and that 'when that cause is removed, simply by the operation of abolishing it, as the origin and agent of the treason that is without justification and without parallel, we shall henceforth be united, be only one country, having only one hope, one ambition, and one destiny.'"

Finally, the group separated. Nicolay remembered, "Speech-making finally came to an end, and such of the visitors as were blessed with friends or good luck sought the retirement of their rooms, where in spite of brass-bands and glee-clubs, and the restless tramping of the less fortunate along the sidewalks, they slept the slumber of mental, added to physical, weariness."

The Wills House

The office in the Wills House

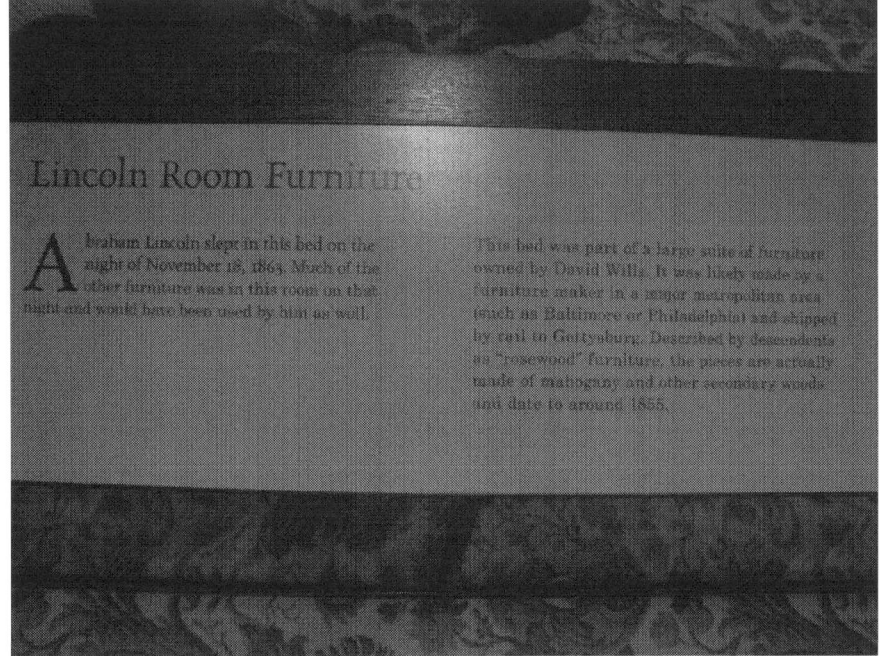

Pictures of the room Lincoln used in the Wills House

Chapter 5: Delivering the Speech

"Gettysburg was an unlovely place on November 19, 1863. The trees, shorn of their limbs, gave evidence of the fearful struggle which had occurred there. The symmetry of the burial acres, with its semi-circular arrangement of lots, was entirely lost in the uneven newly made mounds with their crude markers. Interments were still being made as hastily prepared graves were being discovered from day to day. These physical surroundings contributed much to the solemnness of the gathering. The speakers' platform added little to the decorative features of the occasion. It was forty feet square and stood on the site now occupied by the Gettysburg National Monument. The platform faced away from the cemetery, however, so that the people assembled to hear the program would not be standing on that portion of the grounds where the soldiers were buried. The day itself, however, was a beautiful one and this contributed much to the comfort of the people. But the brightness of the sun only accentuated the ugliness of the place which is now so beautiful and serene." - Louis A. Warren, *Little Known Facts About the Gettysburg Address*

The next morning, the day dawned bright and clear, with just a nip of cold in the air. Lamon recalled, "It was after the breakfast hour on the morning of the 19th that the writer, Mr. Lincoln's private secretary, went to the upper room in the house of Mr. Wills which Mr. Lincoln occupied, to report for duty, and remained with the President while he finished writing the Gettysburg address, during the short leisure he could utilize for this purpose before being called to take his place in the procession, which was announced on the program to move promptly at ten o'clock."

The festivities began with a procession of important officials and dignitaries headed for the new cemetery, and perhaps the most definitive description of this was recorded by William Rathbone in 1938. During an oral history interview, he said, perhaps a bit idealistically, "Because, as a schoolboy, I was in the little town of Gettysburg in Pennsylvania some 75 years ago, I am privileged to tell you today what I then heard and saw when Abraham Lincoln, the wartime president of the United States, delivered his immortal address at the dedication of the national cemetery. When it was known that on a certain day in November, four months after the battle, that President Lincoln, 'Old Abe' as we boys affectionately called him, was to be in Gettysburg, I was excused from my duties at school and accompanied my family at least to see the president and perhaps to hear what he had to say. Bright and early the next morning, I was in the center square of the town where the procession was to form on the cemetery hill where the speaking was to take place. At the head of the procession, preceded by a mounted military band, the first I had ever seen, rode the president. He was mounted on a gray horse of medium size, which accentuated his unusual height, his long legs reaching too near the ground for either grace or good horsemanship. The president was escorted to the cemetery by many distinguished officers of the Army, representatives of foreign countries, military and civic organizations and the surging crowds of patriotic citizens estimated at 20,000."

The saddle used by Lincoln to ride to the cemetery on November 19

A picture of the crowd on November 19

Pictures of a Lincoln memorial in the cemetery

The program began with a rendition of "Homage d'uns Heroes" by Adolph Birgfeld that was performed by his own band. Then, the Reverend T. H. Stockton offered an Invocation. Next, the Marine Corp Band, under the direction of Francis Scala, performed a number, after which the Honorable Edward Everett stepped forward to give a nearly 13,000 word speech that lasted about two hours.

Everett's speech, entitled "The Battles of Gettysburg," was followed by the hymn "Consecration Chant," performed by the Baltimore Glee Club. It was only after all of these performances that Lincoln stepped forward for what were listed as "Dedicatory Remarks, by the President of the United States." By this time, according to Lambert, "The procession that had escorted the President to the field had been greatly belated, and after his arrival upon the platform the proceedings were still further delayed, awaiting the arrival of the orator of the day. Mr. Everett's oration, that had been preceded by a prayer of some length and by music, was of two hours' duration, so that when the President spoke it was to an audience that had been standing for nearly four hours. The brevity of the speech, the absence of rhetorical effort, and its very simplicity prevented its full appreciation."

According to the accepted record of the next two minutes, Lincoln made the following remarks, barely more than 250 words:

> "Four score and seven years ago our fathers brought forth on this continent a new nation, conceived in liberty, and dedicated to the proposition that all men are created equal.
>
> "Now we are engaged in a great civil war, testing whether that nation, or any nation so conceived and so dedicated, can long endure. We are met on a great battlefield of that war. We have come to dedicate a portion of that field, as a final resting place for those who here gave their lives that that nation might live. It is altogether fitting and proper that we should do this.
>
> "But, in a larger sense, we cannot dedicate, we cannot consecrate, we cannot hallow this ground. The brave men, living and dead, who struggled here, have consecrated it, far above our poor power to add or detract. The world will little note, nor long remember what we say here, but it can never forget what they did here. It is for us the living, rather, to be dedicated here to the unfinished work which they who fought here have thus far so nobly advanced. It is rather for us to be here dedicated to the great task remaining before us—that from these honored dead we take increased devotion to that cause for which they gave the last full measure of devotion—that we here highly resolve that these dead shall not have died in vain—that this nation, under God, shall have a new birth of freedom—and that government of the people, by the people, for the people, shall not perish from the earth."

Rathbone later remembered, "After the long, eloquent oration of Honorable Edward Everett of Massachusetts, conceded to be the most finished orator of his day, Lincoln arose and, with a manner serious almost to sadness, gave his brief address that rang from the hills of Gettysburg, around the world and back many times and will ever continue to reverberate in the hearts and minds of all mankind where freedom, forgiveness, tenderness and strength are cherished. During its delivery, with one or two other lads, I had worked my way onto the platform and wiggled through the crowd in front until I stood within 15 feet of Mr. Lincoln and looked up into his serious face. A rough board platform 4 or 5 feet high had been built from which the president spoke. Across the front, over the rail behind which he stood, was draped the nation's flag, the Stars and Stripes, Old Glory, as the soldiers gallantly called it. Although I listened intently to every word the president uttered and heard it clearly, boylike, I could not recall any of it afterwards. But had any of my companions spoken slightingly of it, there would have been a junior Battle of Gettysburg then and there, for any hint or intimation that Old Abe, as we affectionately called him, was deficient or delinquent in any respect would have meant a scrap, so deep-seated was our youthful loyalty."

Chapter 6: Reactions to the Speech

"Lincoln's words were few, two hundred and sixty-five, to be exact, according to the most dependable stenographic report. James Grant Wilson claims it took 'precisely one hundred and thirty-five seconds' to deliver the message. The President, a few days previous to leaving for Gettysburg had confided to a friend that his address was to be 'short — short — short.' The brevity of the message was not the most surprising characteristic of it, although it is said a photographer who planned to make a picture of Lincoln while speaking had insufficient time to get the camera adjusted before the address was over. The apparent care with which Lincoln had prepared the small part he was to take on the program was the outstanding feature of his efforts. As on occasions of similar dedications, according to Secretary Nicolay, the people were expecting 'a few perfunctory words, the mere formality of official dedication.' A formal statement by the President beginning, 'as President of the United States I hereby, etc.,' would have been appropriate but it was just like Lincoln to make something very beautiful out of a commonplace task. Without comment on what had been said before, without apology for lack of time, in simple and sympathetic words, he consecrated the burial field as 'a final resting place for those who here gave their lives.'" - Louis A. Warren, *Little Known Facts About the Gettysburg Address*

As Lambert astutely observed, part of the reason the history of the Gettysburg Address is still unsettled is the simple fact that it was recognized in hindsight as a masterpiece. As a result, negative perceptions at the time have been overlooked or completely forgotten, even by those who may have initially held such a view: "The Address has been so long and so generally accepted as the highest expression of American oratory, that it is difficult to realize that it ever had less appreciation than now. The testimonies of those who heard the Address delivered differ widely as to the reception given it and as to the impression it made."

For example, Clark Carr analyzed what he heard that day when he came to the battlefield cemetery from Illinois: "His expressions were so plain and homely, without any attempt at rhetorical periods, and his statements were so axiomatic, and, I may say, matter-of-fact, and so simple, that I had no idea that as an address it was anything more than ordinary. … Everyone was impressed with his sincerity and earnestness…. There was one sentence that did deeply affect me — the only one in which the President manifested emotion. With the close of that sentence his lips quivered, and there was a tremor in his voice which I can never forget. … The sentence was, ' The world will little note, nor long remember what we say here, but it can never forget what they did here"

Indeed, many people thought little of the Gettysburg Address in November 1863, including the president himself. Lamon, who stood with those listening to Lincoln that day, wrote of the speech, "After its delivery on the day of commemoration, [Lincoln] expressed deep regret that he had not prepared it with greater care. He said to me on the stand, immediately after concluding the speech: 'Lamon, that speech won't scour! It is a flat failure, and the people are disappointed.'

(The word 'scour' he often used in expressing his positive conviction that a thing lacked merit, or would not stand the test of close criticism or the wear of time.) He seemed deeply concerned about what the people might think of his address; more deeply, in fact, than I had ever seen him on any public occasion. His frank and regretful condemnation of his effort, and more especially his manner of expressing that regret, struck me as somewhat remarkable; and my own impression was deepened by the fact that the orator of the day, Mr. Everett, and Secretary Seward both coincided with Mr. Lincoln in his unfavorable view of its merits."

In analyzing Lincoln's opinion that his speech had not been well received, Lamon noted, "The occasion was solemn, impressive, and grandly historic. The people, it is true, stood apparently spell-bound; and the vast throng was hushed and awed into profound silence while Mr. Lincoln delivered his brief speech. But it seemed to him that this silence and attention to his words arose more from the solemnity of the ceremonies and the awful scenes which gave rise to them, than from anything he had said. He believed that the speech was a failure. He thought so at the time, and he never referred to it afterwards, in conversation with me, without some expression of unqualified regret that he had not made the speech better in every way. On the platform from which Mr. Lincoln delivered his address, and only a moment after it was concluded, Mr. Seward turned to Mr. Everett and asked him what he thought of the President's speech. Mr. Everett replied, 'It is not what I expected from him. I am disappointed.' Then in his turn Mr. Everett asked, 'What do you think of it, Mr. Seward?' The response was, 'He has made a failure, and I am sorry for it. His speech is not equal to him.' Mr. Seward then turned to me and asked, '…what do you think of it?' I answered, 'I am sorry to say that it does not impress me as one of his great speeches.'"

Lamon went on to clarify some of the rumors that had swirled about the speech in the years following its delivery: "In the face of these facts it has been repeatedly published that this speech was received by the audience with loud demonstrations of approval; that 'amid the tears, sobs, and cheers it produced in the excited throng, the orator of the day, Mr. Everett, turned to Mr. Lincoln, grasped his hand and exclaimed, 'I congratulate you on your success!' adding in a transport of heated enthusiasm, 'Ah, Mr. President, how gladly would I give my hundred pages to be the author of your twenty lines!'' Nothing of the kind occurred. It is a slander on Mr. Everett, an injustice to Mr. Lincoln, and a falsification of history. Mr. Everett could not have used the words attributed to him, in the face of his own condemnation of the speech uttered a moment before, without subjecting himself to the charge of being a toady and a hypocrite; and he was neither the one nor the other. As a matter of fact, the silence during the delivery of the speech, and the lack of hearty demonstrations of approval immediately after its close, were taken by Mr. Lincoln as certain proof that it was not well received. In that opinion we all shared. If any person then present saw, or thought he saw, the marvelous beauties of that wonderful speech, as intelligent men in all lands now see and acknowledge them, his superabundant caution closed his lips and stayed his pen. Mr. Lincoln said to me after our return to Washington, 'I tell you…that speech fell on the audience like a wet blanket. I am distressed about it. I ought to have prepared it with more care.' Such continued to be his opinion of that most wonderful of all his platform addresses up to the time of his death."

Lamon concluded his remarks on the subject with the following surprising evaluation: "I state it as a fact, and without fear of contradiction, that this famous Gettysburg speech was not regarded by the audience to whom it was addressed, or by the press and people of the United States, as a production of extraordinary merit, nor was it commented on as such until after the death of its author. Those who look thoughtfully into the history of the matter must own that Mr. Lincoln was, on that occasion, 'wiser than he knew.' He was wiser than his audience, wiser than the great scholars and orators who were associated with him in the events of that solemn day. He had unconsciously risen to a height above the level of even the 'cultured thought' of that period."

On the other hand, there were others present who immediately liked the speech. Congressman Robert Miller was present that day, and a few days later, he wrote, "The tall form of the President appeared on the stand and never before have I seen a crowd so vast and restless, after standing so long, so soon stilled and quieted. Hats were removed and all stood motionless to catch the first words he should utter, and as he slowly, clearly, and without the least sign of embarrassment read and spoke for ten minutes you could not mistake the feeling and sentiment of the vast multitude before him. I am convinced that the speech of the President has fully confirmed and I think will confirm all loyal men and women in the belief that Abraham Lincoln, though he may have made mistakes, is the right man in the right place."

Historian Samuel Bates considered what he heard that day unforgettable: "Its delivery was more solemn and impressive than is possible to conceive from its perusal. Major Harry T. Lee, who was one of the actors in the battle and who was present upon the platform at the dedication, says that the people listened with marked attention throughout the two hours that Mr. Everett spoke; …but that when Mr. Lincoln came forward and, with a voice burdened with emotion, uttered these sublime words the bosoms of that vast audience were lifted as a great wave of the sea ; and that when he came to the passage, ' The brave men living and dead, who struggled here,' there was not a dry eye."

Isaac Arnold agreed: "Before the first sentence was completed, a thrill of feeling like an electric shock pervaded the crowd. That mysterious influence called magnetism, which sometimes so affects a popular assembly, spread to every heart. The vast audience was instantly hushed and hung upon his every word and syllable. Everyone felt that it was not the honored dead only, but the living actor and speaker that the world for all time to come would note and remember, and that the speaker in the thrilling words he was uttering was linking his name forever with the glory of the dead… All his hearers realized that the great actor in the drama stood before them, and that the words he said would live as long as the language; that they were words which would be recollected in all future ages among all peoples, as often as men should be called upon to die for liberty and country. As he closed, and the tears and sobs and cheers which expressed the emotions of the people subsided, he turned to Everett and, grasping his hand, said, ' I congratulate you on your success.' The orator gratefully replied, 'Ah! Mr. President, how gladly would I exchange all my hundred pages to have been the author of your twenty lines.'"

Several decades later, Major Azor Nickerson, who was seated on the dais as Lincoln spoke, recalled, "Others, too, have differed as to the immediate effects of the President's remarks. I give the impressions received at the time, which were also identical with those of all with whom I spoke. I thought then and still think it was the shortest, grandest speech to which I ever listened. ... My own emotions may perhaps be imagined when it is remembered that he was facing the spot where only a short time before we had our death grapple with Pickett's men and he stood almost immediately over the place where I had lain and seen my comrades torn in fragments by the enemy's cannon-balls — think then, if you please, how these words fell upon my ear. ... If at that moment the Supreme Being had appeared with an offer to undo my past life, give back to me a sound body free from the remembrance even of sufferings past and the imminence of those that must necessarily embitter all the years to come, I should have indignantly spurned the offer, such was the effect upon me of this immortal dedication."

A committee of leading citizens from Boston reported back to their home town, "Perhaps nothing in the whole proceedings made so deep an impression on the vast assemblage or has conveyed to the country in so concise a form the lesson of the hour, as the remarks of the President, their simplicity and force make them worthy of a prominence among the utterances from high places."

Another man who heard the Gettysburg Address in person was Joseph L. Grant, a reporter for the Associated Press who wrote that there was "long, continual applause" at the close of the speech. Assuming that both Ward and Grant were telling the truth, the applause may have seemed to Lincoln and the others as only perfunctory, or maybe more in recognition of the occasion than the speech itself.

surrounded the position taken by the immense multitude of people.

The Marshal took up a position on the left of the stand. Numerous flags and banners, suitably draped, were exhibited on the stand among the audience. The entire scene was one of grandeur due to the importance of the occasion. So quiet were the people that every word uttered by the orator of the day must have been heard by them all, notwithstanding the immensity of the concours.

Among the distinguished persons on the platform were the following: Governors Bradford, of Maryland; Curtin, of Pennsylvania; Morton, of Indiana; Seymour, of New-York; Parker, of New-Jersey, and Tod, of Ohio; Ex-Gov. Dennison, of Ohio; John Brough, Governor Elect, of Ohio; Charles Anderson, Lieutenant-Governor of Ohio; Major-Generals Schenck, Stahel, Doubleday, and Couch; Brigadier-General Gibbon; and Provost-Marshal-General Fry.

PRESIDENT LINCOLN'S ADDRESS.

The President then delivered the following dedicatory speech:

Fourscore and seven years ago our Fathers brought forth upon this Continent a new nation, conceived in liberty and dedicated to the proposition that all men are created equal. [Applause.] Now we are engaged in a great civil war, testing whether that nation, or any nation so conceived and so dedicated, can long endure. We are met on a great battle-field of that war. We are met to dedicate a portion of it as the final resting-place of those who here gave their lives that that nation might live. It is altogether fitting and proper that we should do this. But in a larger sense we cannot dedicate. We cannot consecrate, we cannot hallow this ground. The brave men, living and dead, who struggled here have consecrated it far above our power to add or detract. [Applause.] The world will little note nor long remember, what we say here, but it can never forget what they did here. [Applause.] It is for us, the living, rather to be dedicated here to the refinished work that they have thus so far nobly carried on. [Applause.] It is rather for us to be here dedicated to the great task remaining before us, that from these honored dead we take increased devotion to that cause for which they here gave the last full measure of devotion; that we here highly resolve that the dead shall not have died in vain; [applause] that the Nation shall under God have a new birth of freedom, and that Governments of the people, by the people and for the people, shall not perish from the earth. [Long continued applause.]

Three cheers were then given for the President and the Governors of the States.

After the delivery of the addresses, the dirge and the benediction closed the exercises, and the immense assemblage separated at about 4 o'clock.

The *New York Times* report seems to match Grant's assessment of the applause

As is often the case, not everyone had the same recollection. John Russell Young, who also sat on the platform with Lincoln, remembered that reports claimed the speech "was studded with applause, but I do not remember the applause and am afraid the appreciative reporter was more than generous — may have put in the applause himself as a personal expression of opinion. ... I have read…of the emotions produced by the President's address, the transcendent awe that fell upon everyone who heard those most mighty and ever living words, to be remembered with pride through the ages, I have read of the tears that fell and the solemn hush, as though in a cathedral solemnity in the most holy moment of the Sacrifice. ... There was nothing of this, to the writer at least, in the Gettysburg Address."

While Lincoln's Gettysburg Address might not have made much of an impact on those who were not there, at least according to Lamon, is was a big hit in Europe. Lamon noted, "The marvelous perfection, the intrinsic excellence of the Gettysburg speech as a masterpiece of English composition, seem to have escaped the scrutiny of even the most scholarly critics of that day, on this side of the Atlantic. That discovery was made, it must be regretfully owned, by distinguished writers on the other side. The London 'Spectator,' the 'Saturday Review,' the 'Edinburgh Review,' and some other European journals were the first to discover, or at least to proclaim, the classical merits of the Gettysburg speech. It was then that we began to realize that it was indeed a masterpiece; and it dawned upon many minds that we had entertained an angel unawares, who had left us unappreciated."

The following day, one newspaper observed in an article entitled, "The Gettysburg Solemnities": "The proceedings at Gettysburg yesterday seem to have been, in every respect, appropriate. The presence of the President and many other distinguished men, together with a vast multitude of people from all parts of the country, shows how high is the popular estimate of the victory that was won by General Meade in July. It shows, too, how dearly the nation treasures the memories of the brave men who laid down their lives on those memorable days. Mr. Everett's oration is a fine, scholarly production. It is somewhat deficient in warmth, as is all that he writes; but it will serve as an enduring record, not merely of the dedication of the National Cemetery, but of the whole campaign which was crowned with victory at Gettysburg. The President's brief speech of dedication Is most happily expressed. It is warm, earnest, unaffected and touching. Thousands who would not read the long, elaborate oration of Mr. Everett will read the President's words, and not many of them will do it without a moistening of the eyes and a swelling of the heart. The really sacred soil of the battlefield of Gettysburg has now been solemnly set apart as the resting place of its heroes, and it will attract pilgrims from all parts of the land as long as we are a nation."

In a rare twist, that writer's prophetic words about both the speeches and the battlefield proved to be completely accurate.

Chapter 7: The Real Climax of All American Eloquence

"EDWARD EVERETT, principal speaker at the dedication, wrote to the President the day following the exercises and complimented him on the timeliness of his remarks. Everett said in part: 'Permit me also to express my great admiration of the thoughts expressed by you, with such eloquent simplicity and appropriateness, at the consecration of the Cemetery. I should be glad if I could flatter myself that I came as near the central idea of the occasion in two hours as you did in two minutes.' Lincoln's reply was as gracious as Mr. Everett's compliment. He wrote: 'I am pleased to know that in your judgment the little I did say was not entirely a failure. I knew Mr. Everett would not fail.' Mr. Everett did not fail in Lincoln's opinion, and more than a year later he was praising the words of Everett at Gettysburg. It is doubtful if Lincoln was ever conscious of the fact that his own Gettysburg Address was the real climax of all American eloquence." - Louis A. Warren, *Little Known Facts About the Gettysburg Address*

While Lincoln is famous for having been largely self-educated, he was a voracious reader with a keen mind, and after becoming more financially (and politically) successful, he had access to many of the classical works of literature. Therefore it is not surprising that he drew upon a number of sources to craft America's most famous speech.

For instance, historian Louis Warren noted similarities between the Gettysburg Address and Pericles' Funeral Oration during the Peloponnesian War as recounted by Thucydides. Warren explained, "Only one other great oration has been compared favorably with that of Lincoln at Gettysburg. That is the funeral oration by the immortal Pericles at Athens. There are many striking similarities in these two speeches. Both were delivered where brave men had fallen in battle. In Greece, Athenians had fought against Spartans, North against South, Greek against Greek. In America, the ground was where Puritan grappled with Cavalier, North faced the South, and American met American. Both Lincoln and Pericles began their orations with direct references to the contributions of the fathers.' Pericles began, 'I will begin then with our ancestors, our fathers inherited, etc.' Lincoln opened with, 'Four score and seven years ago, our fathers, etc.' It is significant that both orators, separated in time by centuries, should begin by commemorating the works of the fathers."

Then there was the issue of "government of the people, by the people, for the people." Warren noted, "Oft times a gem needs but the proper setting to bring out its brilliancy and full worth. Government of, by, and for the people was no new idea conceived by Abraham Lincoln, but he placed this jewel of democratic idealism as a crowning thought within the most eloquent oration of modern days. Five years before Gettysburg, Lincoln acquired two pamphlets containing addresses by Theodore Parker, delivered in 1858. In one of Parker's speeches, Lincoln underlined this statement: 'Democracy — The All Man Power; government over all, by all, and for the sake of all.' The other pamphlet contained a sermon delivered by Parker in Music Hall, Boston, on July 4, 1858, and these words Lincoln enclosed with a pencil: 'Democracy is Direct Self-Government over all the people, for all the people, by all the people.' Lincoln may have read in many instances statements which conveyed the thought with which he brought the Gettysburg Address to a close, but this slogan of a free people never had been spoken with more feeling, nor uttered in a more inspirational atmosphere, than on the nineteenth of November, 1863: 'That this nation, under God, shall have a new birth of freedom — and that government of the people, by the people, for the people, shall not perish from the earth.'"

Parker

In his evaluation of that particular phrase, Lamon wrote, "For using in his Gettysburg speech the celebrated phrase, 'the government of the people, by the people, and for the people,' Mr. Lincoln has been subjected to the most brutal criticism as well as to the most groundless flattery. Some have been base enough to insinuate against that great and sincere man that he was guilty of the crime of wilful plagiarism; others have ascribed to him the honor of originating the phrase entire. There is injustice to him in either view of the case. I personally know that Mr. Lincoln made no pretense of originality in the matter; nor was he, on the other hand, conscious of having appropriated the thought, or even the exact words, of any other man. If he is subject to the charge of plagiarism, so is the great Webster, who used substantially the same phrase in his celebrated reply to Hayne. Both men may have acquired the peculiar form of expression (the thought itself being as old as the republican idea of government) by the process known as unconscious appropriation. Certain it is that neither Lincoln nor Webster originated the phrase. Let us see how the case stands."

For his part, Lamon gave more credit to Parker: "In an address before the New England Antislavery Convention in Boston, May 29, 1850, Theodore Parker defined Democracy as 'a government of all the people, by all the people, for all the people, of course,' which language is identical with that employed by Mr. Lincoln in his Gettysburg speech. Substantially the same phrase was used by Judge Joel Parker in the Massachusetts Constitutional Convention in 1853. A distinguished diplomat has acquainted me with the singular fact that almost the identical phrase employed by Mr. Lincoln was used in another language by a person whose existence even was not probably known to Mr. Webster, the Parkers, or to Mr. Lincoln. On the thirty-first page of a work entitled 'Geschichte der Schweizerischen Regeneration von 1830 bis 1848, von P. Feddersen,' appears an account of a public meeting held at Olten, Switzerland, in May, 1830. On that occasion a speaker named Schinz used the following language, as translated by my friend just referred to: 'All the governments of Switzerland [referring to the cantons] must acknowledge that they are simply from all the people, by all the people, and for all the people. These extracts are enough to show that no American statesman or writer can lay claim to the origin or authorship of the phrase in question. No friend of Mr. Lincoln will pretend that it is the coinage of his fertile brain; nor will any fair-minded man censure him for using it as he did in his Gettysburg speech. As a phrase of singular compactness and force, it was employed by him, legitimately and properly, as a fitting conclusion to an address which the judgment of both hemispheres has declared will live as a model of classic oratory while free government shall continue to be known and revered among men."

William Herndon, Lincoln's partner in his Illinois law firm, also noted Parker's influence: "I brought with me additional sermons and lectures of Theodore Parker, who was warm in his commendation of Lincoln. One of these was a lecture on 'The Effect of Slavery on the American People' ... which I gave to Lincoln, who read and returned it. He liked especially the following expression, which he marked with a pencil, and which he in substance afterwards used in his Gettysburg Address: 'Democracy is direct self-government, over all the people, for all the people, by all the people.'"

Chief Justice John Marshall had written something similar decades earlier in the landmark case of *McCulloch v. Maryland* (1819): "The government of the Union, then (whatever may be the influence of this fact on the case), is, emphatically and truly, a government of the people. In form, and in substance, it emanates from them. Its powers are granted by them, and are to be exercised directly on them, and for their benefit."

As it turned out, the phrase pre-dated all of those men, for when John Wycliffe first translated the Bible into English in 1384, he prefaced his work with the statement, "This Bible is for the government of the people, for the people and by the people."

Another intriguing phrase in the address is "Under God." Warren observed, "ALL public speakers are aware that there comes to one spontaneously, on occasions of unusual emotional experiences, expressions which may have been lying dormant for years, apparently waiting for the proper moment to find voice. Lincoln's preliminary draft of the Gettysburg Address makes no mention of Deity, and this has been made a great point by those who would prefer to have it so. Every stenographic report of what Lincoln actually said, however, puts in the expression "under God" as having been spoken by the President. Back in Lincoln's childhood days, he had been greatly impressed by Weems' story of George Washington and he was able to quote many passages from this inspirational biography. Weems had one expression which he frequently used in his book, a word couplet — "under God." It was in the midst of Lincoln's final declaration that these two words sprang forth to hallow the entire address with the atmosphere of reverence."

The problem with the phrase "Under God" is that it did not appear any either of the first two drafts of his speech that Lincoln wrote before he gave it. However, it did appear in many of the published versions of the speech, including those taken from records made in short hand by stenographers during his address. Historian William Barton accepts that the stenographers were accurate in this case: "Every stenographic report, good, bad and indifferent, says 'that the nation shall, under God, have a new birth of freedom.' There was no common source from which all the reporters could have obtained those words but from Lincoln's own lips at the time of delivery. It will not do to say that [Secretary of War] Stanton suggested those words after Lincoln's return to Washington, for the words were telegraphed by at least three reporters on the afternoon of the delivery."

Lincoln also included it in later versions of the speech that he hand wrote at the request of others. Therefore, it seems most likely that, while it was not part of his original plan, he felt moved by the spirit of the moment to add the phrase while he was speaking. Ronald White, a professor religious history, asserted, "It was an uncharacteristically spontaneous revision for a speaker who did not trust extemporaneous speech. Lincoln had added impromptu words in several earlier speeches, but always offered a subsequent apology for the change. In this instance, he did not. And Lincoln included 'under God' in all three copies of the address he prepared at later dates. 'Under God' pointed backward and forward: back to 'this nation', which drew its breath from both political and religious sources, but also forward to a 'new birth'. Lincoln had come to see the Civil War as a ritual of purification. The old Union had to die. The old man had to die. Death became a transition to a new Union and a new humanity."

Chapter 8: Different Versions

"Five different versions of the Gettysburg address, strange to say, were all written or spoken by Abraham Lincoln, and there may have been others equally authentic. They can be identified as (1) preliminary writings, (2) spoken words, and (3) revisory copies. One author has put it like this, 'What he intended to say, what he said, what he wished he had said.' It is apparent that one copy of the address, and this one is also revised, by the way, was written preliminary to the delivery of the speech. There is no way of learning how many revisions the speech underwent before it finally was delivered. The most dependable record of what Lincoln actually said seems to have been made by a member of the Boston commission who went to Gettysburg, instructed to take down in shorthand the words of the President. This he did and his transcription was not jumbled by telegraph operators or rapid fire typesetters but was carefully and accurately prepared to be included in the commissioner's report. After the dedication, copies of Lincoln's address were requested by Edward Everett, George Bancroft, and probably others. The writing which he prepared for Everett and the two copies he wrote for Bancroft have been preserved. It is the version in the final Bancroft copy that is most widely used, and it has become known as the authentic Gettysburg Address of Abraham Lincoln." - Louis A. Warren, *Little Known Facts About the Gettysburg Address*

One of the things that makes analyzing the Gettysburg Address so challenging is that fact that there are at least five known versions of Lincoln's famous remarks, each with its own variations, critics and defenders. The first of these is the Nicolay Manuscript, considered by many to be the first draft of the speech, but over the next several decades, controversy raged over which manuscript matched the actual speech given at Gettysburg in November 1863. In 1909, the *Washington Star* reported, "That has been a matter of friendly controversy among interested parties almost from the day of its delivery. Among those who took part in this discussion were John Hay, former secretary of state, and John G. Nicolay, both of whom were secretaries to President Lincoln; Robert T. Lincoln, his surviving son; J. P. Nicholson, chairman of the Gettysburg National Military Park Commission; Gen. Aleshire, quarter master general; Gen. Oliver, assistant secretary of war, and many others. From the mass of correspondence on the subject it appears that there are three sources of authority for Lincoln's Gettysburg address, or rather three versions of it. They are all identical in thought, but differ slightly in expression."

For his part, Nicolay described the three versions mentioned as follows:

"1. The original autograph MS.[manuscript] draft, written by Mr. Lincoln partly at Washington and partly at Gettysburg. [Nicolay]

2. The version made by the shorthand reporter on the stand at Gettysburg when the President delivered It. which was telegraphed and was printed in the leading newspapers of the country on the following morning.

3. The revised copy made by the President a few days after his return to Washington, upon a careful comparison of his original draft and the printed newspaper version, with his own recollection of the exact form in which he delivered it." [Hay]

According to Lambert, "Nicolay says that the President did not read from the written pages, and that he did not deliver the Address in the form in which it was first written, but from the fulness of thought and memory rounded it out nearly to its final rhetorical completeness. Brooks states that as Mr. Lincoln read from the manuscript he made a few verbal changes. Comparison of the several reports named leads to the conclusion that the President, remembering what he had written in the Hay manuscript, delivered his Address in closer accordance with it than with the Nicolay manuscript which he held, but to which he referred little. The North American report, which in my judgment reproduces the words spoken more accurately than any other, and more closely than the President's final revision, differs from the Hay manuscript in several instances, but materially only in the words ' under God,' which were interpolated by the President as he spoke, for the phrase does not appear either in the Nicolay or the Hay manuscript, and in the use of 'the' instead of 'this' before 'government of the people.'"

In explaining how this happened, Lambert claimed, "Nicolay says that a few days after the visit to Gettysburg, upon receipt from Mr. Wills of a request on behalf of the States interested in the National Cemetery for the original manuscript of the Dedication Address, the President reexamined his original draft and the version that had appeared in the newspapers, and he saw that because of the variations between them, the first, that is, the Nicolay, seemed incomplete and the others imperfect; he therefore directed his secretaries to make copies of the several reports of the Associated Press and, ' comparing these with his original draft and with his own fresh recollection of the form in which he delivered it, he made a new autograph copy, a careful and deliberate revision.' What became of this first revision is unknown, it was not received by Mr. Wills, who wrote me years ago: 'I did not make a copy of my report of President Lincoln's speech at Gettysburg from a transcript from the original, but from one of the press reports. I have since always used the revised copy furnished the Baltimore fair, of which I have a facsimile in lithograph.'"

The final version mentioned is likely the Hay Copy. According to Lambert, "Another manuscript exists, which is now in the possession of the family of the late John Hay, who as one of the President's private secretaries was present at the dedication. This manuscript, which is in the President's autograph, is reproduced in facsimile in Putnam's Magazine for February, 1909, in connection with 'Recollections of Lincoln' by Gen. James Grant Wilson, who believes the manuscript was written after the President's return from Gettysburg. The Hay manuscript is undoubtedly the second existing draft of the address, but because of information obtained from Col. John P. Nicholson, to whom it was imparted by Secretary Hay, I am convinced that this manuscript was written before November 19, 1863, and that it was inadvertently left at Washington. This opinion is further strengthened by the internal evidence of the manuscript itself."

A picture of the Hay copy with Lincoln's revisions marked in it

Note that the first and third copies mentioned here were in Lincoln's own hand. A third copy, also written by Lincoln, was sent to Everett at the latter's request. Nicolay added, "The last of these, is the regular outgrowth of the two which preceded it and is the perfected product of the President's rhetorical and literary mastery."

Of course, the biggest problem stemming from the existence of the different copies is that they are far from identical, even among those written by Lincoln himself. Lambert explained, "The variations between the several contemporary versions of the Address and its many subsequent reproductions are remarkable, particularly in view of its brevity and importance. Attention has more than once been attracted to these variations; and because of the differences between the earlier reports and the version published in autographic facsimile in 1864, it has been assumed that the discrepancies were due either to blunders on the part of reporters, or to their attempts to improve the President's composition. But examination of a number of versions forces the conclusion that while some of the minor variations in the newspaper reports were caused by typographical or telegraphic errors, the rhetorical differences between these reports and the later version were plainly the result of the author's own revision. The reports of the Address, published November 20, 1863, in the Ledger, the North American, the Press, and the Bulletin of this city, in the Tribune and the Herald of New York, in the Advertiser and the Journal of Boston, and in the Springfield Republican, and on the 23d in the Cincinnati Commercial, were furnished by the Associated Press. The reports printed in the Philadelphia papers named agree with the exception of obvious misprints. The New York papers agree with a single exception, probably a typographical error; the Boston papers also agree substantially with but three verbal variations. But the respective versions of the several cities differ from each other in a number of details, probably because of errors in telegraphing the reports from Gettysburg."

For a while, it didn't really matter which version of the Gettysburg Address was seen as the most accurate, but by the turn of the 20th century, there had developed a move across the country to have the Gettysburg Address inscribed on various plaques on buildings and in military cemeteries. At this point, the Quartermaster General of the United States was tasked with deciding which version should be used, and he narrowed his choices down in 1909:

> "1. The final revision published in *Autograph Leaves of Our Country's Authors*,' prepared by President Lincoln five months after the address for the soldiers' and sailors' fair at Baltimore. This is a version desired by both Col. Nicholson and Robert T. Lincoln. The latter regarded it as representing his father's last and best thoughts as to the address. [Lincoln handwrote two more copies of the Address to be used for this project. They are known as the Bancroft Copy and the Bliss Copy]
>
> 2. The version stipulated to be used by the act of Feb. 11, 1895, appropriating $5,000 for the bronze tablet containing the address to be erected in the Gettysburg National Park. This differs slightly from the Baltimore Version.
>
> 3. The John Hay version, from a photographic facsimile of the original manuscript as written and corrected by President Lincoln four days after he had delivered the address and presented it to John Hay. This differs in several particulars from either of the above versions."

The Quartermaster General ultimately decided to pass the buck: "In view of the discrepancies which appear in the several versions of this address, the matter is resubmitted with the request for a decision as to the one which shall be used for the tablets in the national cemeteries."

Then there was the matter of the differences in the versions published in newspapers across the country. As Lambert pointed out, "The reports of the Address published in the Philadelphia Inquirer and in the Cincinnati Gazette, November 20 and 21 respectively, differ materially from each other and from the Associated Press report, and are apparently independent in source ; lacking in completeness, they seem to be paraphrases rather than literal reports, and are probably free renderings of notes made at the time, but are valuable so far as they go, in aiding to determine which of the other reports most nearly represents the words actually spoken. Another independent report of greater value is that made by the Massachusetts Commissioners, which they assert is " in the correct form as the words actually spoken by the President, with great deliberation, were taken down by one of" themselves. The differences between their report and that printed in the North American, which is freer from obvious errors than any other version of the Associated Press report that I have seen, are slight."

Without the debate being definitively settled, the controversy continued. Colonel J. P. Nicholson, then chairman of the Gettysburg National Park Commission, complained to the Quartermaster General: "We are not aware of the source from which the address was obtained in the act creating the National Park, but, word for word, it follows the Baltimore version. The punctuation, however, is the work of the public printer, and is in accordance with the rules of punctuation followed in his office. Colonel Lincoln [Abraham Lincoln's only surviving son, Robert] is undoubtedly correct in his contention of the manner in which the address should be printed, and the Baltimore version as given in the 'Autograph Leaves' should be used and none other. As no tablet has been cast for the Gettysburg National Park there is none to change. When it is cast for the park it will follow, with the approval of the Secretary of War, the Baltimore version."

Robert Lincoln, Lincoln's eldest son and the only one to reach adulthood, also weighed in. He wrote to the Quartermaster General, "As I wrote you before, the Baltimore fair version represents my father's last and best thought as to the address, and the corrections in it were legitimate for an author, and I think there is no doubt they improve the version as written out for Col. Hay. And, as I said to you before, I earnestly hope that the Baltimore fair version will be used. It differs, as you indicate, very slightly from your exhibit A. which, as you say, is given in the statutes-at-large, making an appropriation for the tablet at the Gettysburg National Cemetery. But the statute version was not made, of course, by any responsible person, and I think its incorrections should not be perpetuated when we have, as I have indicated, an exact thing to go by. I am quite sure as a lawyer that there is no obligation upon you, in the new tablets you are making to follow the errors in the text in this old statute, and I trust that you will not do so. I have before me as I write, the book published by the Baltimore Sanitary Fair, which contains a full-sized lithographic reproduction of the address as my father sent to the fair to be used for its benefit."

Finally, the Secretary of War decided that the Baltimore Fair Version of the Gettysburg Address would become and remain the official version "for use on all the tablets to be erected in the national cemeteries as well as for the proposed memorial at Gettysburg. It is proposed to place the latter tablet as near as possible to the exact spot where the martyred President stood when he delivered the address."

Nevertheless, the importance of the Gettysburg Address and the brevity has ensured that people are still obsessed with determining the words exactly as Lincoln delivered them. As Lambert pointed out, "In an address so brief, but so momentous, every syllable tells; and though the differences between the final revision and the speech as actually delivered are few and seemingly immaterial, the changes intensify its strength and pathos and add to its beauty, and as so revised the speech cannot be too jealously preserved as the ultimate expression of the author's sublime thought. Increasing appreciation of Lincoln's character and of his fitness for the great work to which in the providence of God he was called enhances the value of his every word, and surely the form by which he intended this utterance should be judged is that in which we should perpetuate the Gettysburg Address."

Online Resources

The Greatest Battles in History: The Battle of Gettysburg by Charles River Editors

The History of the Civil War: The Causes, Battles, and Generals of the War Between the States by Charles River Editors

Bibliography

Barton, William E. (1950). *Lincoln at Gettysburg: What He Intended to Say; What He Said; What he was Reported to have Said; What he Wished he had Said.* New York: Peter Smith.

Boritt, Gabor (2006). *The Gettysburg Gospel: The Lincoln Speech That Nobody Knows* Simon & Schuster.

Gramm, Kent. (2001) *November: Lincoln's Elegy at Gettysburg.* Bloomington: Indiana University Press.

Kunhardt, Philip B., Jr. (1983) *A New Birth of Freedom: Lincoln at Gettysburg.* Little Brown & Co.

Reid, Ronald F. "Newspaper Responses to the Gettysburg Addresses". *Quarterly Journal of Speech* 1967 53(1): 50–60.

White, Ronald C. Jr. (2005) *The Eloquent President: A Portrait of Lincoln Through His Words.* New York: Random House. Wills, Garry. (1992) *Lincoln at Gettysburg: The Words That Remade America.* New York: Simon and Schuster.